Christmas
AF601329
3D
Tom and Becky
will tell us
a Christmas story

Call to order: 916-715-0442
www.3d.lovelylivebooks.com/gifts

Xulon Press
2301 Lucien Way #415
Maitland, FL 32751
407.339.4217
www.xulonpress.com

Printed in the United States of America.

ISBN-13: 978-1-54564-899-5

«Christmas». 2016. No expiration date.
Quotes are given in accordance with the New Living Translation.
Graphic Designer: A. Zaitsev, Artists: Kardakov S. Zolotov A.

Instructions for installing the application

To download a mobile app for iPhone, iPad and Android smartphone, scan the QR code on the left. Or the App Store (for iPhone and iPad) and the portal Google Play (for Android), type in the search word bluegg.

Install the mobile app «3D Christmas» on your mobile device.

When you first launch the app, point the camera at a bar code label located on the right license and complete the registration "Internet Wi-Fi is necessary," but then internet is not necessary.

Download on your smartphone or tablet a free mobile application «3D Christmas», point your smartphone camera at a special marker on the pages of the book - and go ahead! Direct your device on the page and characters - Tom and Becky will be a virtual 3D, and then touch the Characters. Help Tom find out more about Christmas, and you will better understand the value of this wonderful holiday!

This is how Jesus the Messiah was born.
His mother, Mary, was engaged
to be married to Joseph. But before
the marriage took place, while she was still
a virgin, she became pregnant through the
power of the Holy Spirit. Joseph, her fiance,
was a good man and did not want to disgrace
her publicly, so he decided
to break the engagement quietly.

Matthew 1:18-19

Read
the text
on the page

Look at
the picture
on your left

Point your
camera on
the marker

Help Tom
understand
the story

As he considered this, an angel of the Lord appeared to him in a dream. "Joseph, son of David," the angel said, "do not be afraid to take Mary as your wife. For the child within her was conceived by the Holy Spirit. And she will have a son, and you are to name him Jesus, for he will save his people from their sins."

All of this occurred to fulfill the Lord's message through his prophet:

"Look! The virgin will conceive a child!
She will give birth to a son,
and they will call him Immanuel,
which means 'God is with us.'"

When Joseph woke up, he did as the angel of the Lord commanded and took Mary as his wife. But he did not have sexual relations with her until her son was born. And Joseph named him Jesus.

Matthew 1:20-25

At that time the Roman emperor, Augustus, decreed that a census should be taken throughout the Roman Empire. (This was the first census taken when Quirinius was governor of Syria.) All returned to their own ancestral towns to register for this census. And because Joseph was a descendant of King David, he had to go to Bethlehem in Judea, David's ancient home. He traveled there from the village of Nazareth in Galilee. He took with him Mary, his fiancé, who was now obviously pregnant. And while they were there, the time came for her baby to be born.

Luke 2:1-6

That night there were shepherds staying in the fields nearby, guarding their flocks of sheep. Suddenly, an angel of the Lord appeared among them, and the radiance of the Lord's glory surrounded them. They were terrified, but the angel reassured them. "Don't be afraid!" he said. "I bring you good news that will bring great joy to all people. The Savior — yes, the Messiah, the Lord — has been born today in Bethlehem, the city of David! And you will recognize him by this sign: You will find a baby wrapped snugly in strips of cloth, lying in a manger."

Suddenly, the angel was joined by a vast host of others — the armies of heaven — praising God and saying,

"Glory to God in highest heaven,
and peace on earth to those with whom God is pleased."

When the angels had returned to heaven, the shepherds said to each other, "Let's go to Bethlehem! Let's see this thing that has happened, which the Lord has told us about."

Luke 2:8-15

Read the text on the page

Look at the picture on your left

Point your camera on the marker

Help Tom understand the story

They hurried to the village and found Mary and Joseph. And there was the baby, lying in the manger. After seeing him, the shepherds told everyone what had happened and what the angel had said to them about this child. All who heard the shepherds' story were astonished, but Mary kept all these things in her heart and thought about them often. The shepherds went back to their flocks, glorifying and praising God for all they had heard and seen. It was just as the angel had told them

Luke 2:16-20

Read the text on the page

Look at the picture on your left

Point your camera on the marker

Help Tom understand the story

Jesus was born in Bethlehem in Judea, during the reign of King Herod. About that time some wise men from eastern lands arrived in Jerusalem, asking, "Where is the newborn king of the Jews? We saw his star as it rose, and we have come to worship him."

King Herod was deeply disturbed when he heard this, as was everyone in Jerusalem. He called a meeting of the leading priests and teachers of religious law and asked, "Where is the Messiah supposed to be born?"

"In Bethlehem in Judea," they said, "for this is what the prophet wrote:

'And you, O Bethlehem in the land of Judah, are not least among the ruling cities of Judah, for a ruler will come from you who will be the shepherd for my people Israel.'"

Then Herod called for a private meeting with the wise men, and he learned from them the time when the star first appeared. Then he told them, "Go to Bethlehem and search carefully for the child. And when you find him, come back and tell me so that I can go and worship him, too!"

Matthew 2:1-8

After this interview the wise men went their way. And the star they had seen in the east guided them to Bethlehem. It went ahead of them and stopped over the place where the child was. When they saw the star, they were filled with joy!

Matthew 2:9-10

Look at
the picture
on your left

Point your
camera on
the marker

Help Tom
understand
the story

They entered the house and saw the child with his mother, Mary, and they bowed down and worshiped him. Then they opened their treasure chests and gave him gifts of gold, frankincense, and myrrh.

When it was time to leave, they returned to their own country by another route, for God had warned them in a dream not to return to Herod.

Matthew 2:11-12

After the wise men were gone, an angel of the Lord appeared to Joseph in a dream. "Get up! Flee to Egypt with the child and his mother," the angel said. "Stay there until I tell you to return, because Herod is going to search for the child to kill him."
That night Joseph left for Egypt with the child and Mary, his mother, and they stayed there until Herod's death. This fulfilled what the Lord had spoken through the prophet: "I called my Son out of Egypt."

Matthew 2:13-15

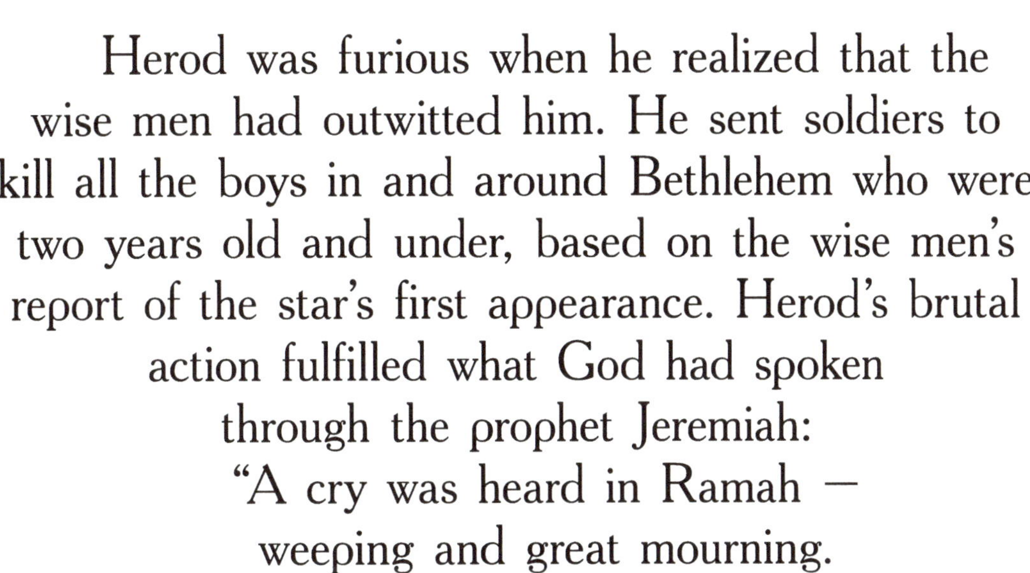

Herod was furious when he realized that the wise men had outwitted him. He sent soldiers to kill all the boys in and around Bethlehem who were two years old and under, based on the wise men's report of the star's first appearance. Herod's brutal action fulfilled what God had spoken through the prophet Jeremiah:

"A cry was heard in Ramah –
weeping and great mourning.
Rachel weeps for her children,
refusing to be comforted,
for they are dead."

Matthew 2:16-18

Read the text on the page

Look at the picture on your left

Point your camera on the marker

Help Tom understand the story

When Herod died, an angel of the Lord appeared in a dream to Joseph in Egypt. “Get up!” the angel said. “Take the child and his mother back to the land of Israel, because those who were trying to kill the child are dead.”

So Joseph got up and returned to the land of Israel with Jesus and his mother. But when he learned that the new ruler of Judea was Herod’s son Archelaus, he was afraid to go there. Then, after being warned in a dream, he left for the region of Galilee. So the family went and lived in a town called Nazareth. This fulfilled what the prophets had said: “He will be called a Nazarene.”

Matthew 2:19-23

Silent night, holy night
All is calm, all is bright
Round yon Virgin Mother and Child
Holy Infant so tender and mild
Sleep in heavenly peace
Sleep in heavenly peace
Silent night, holy night!
Shepherds quake at the sight
Glories stream from heaven afar
Heavenly hosts sing «Alleluia»!
Christ, the Saviour is born
Christ, the Saviour is born
Silent night, holy night
Son of God, love's pure light
Radiant beams from Thy holy face
With the dawn of redeeming grace
Jesus, Lord,...

www.ingramcontent.com/pod-product-compliance
Ingram Content Group UK Ltd.
Pitfield, Milton Keynes, MK11 3LW, UK
UKHW060117300726
14090UKWH00002B/249

* 9 7 8 1 5 4 5 6 4 8 9 9 5 *